How does a VOLCANO become an ISLAND?

Linda Tagliaferro

Chicago, Illinois

www.heinemannraintree.com
Visit our website to find out
more information about
Heinemann-Raintree books.

To order:

☎ Phone 888-454-2279

💻 Visit www.heinemannraintree.com
to browse our catalog and order online.

Edited by David Andrews and Laura Knowles
Designed by Richard Parker and Wagtail
Original illustrations © Capstone Global Library, LLC 2010
Illustrated by Jeff Edwards
Picture research by Mica Brancic
Originated by Modern Age Repro House Ltd
Printed and Bound in the United States
by Corporate Graphics

14 13 12 11 10
10 9 8 7 6 5 4 3 2 1

Library of Congress Cataloging-in-Publication Data
Tagliaferro, Linda.
  How does a volcano become an island? / Linda Tagliaferro.
    p. cm. -- (How does it happen?)
  Includes bibliographical references and index.
  ISBN 978-1-4109-3447-5 (hc) -- ISBN 978-1-4109-3455-0
(pb)
  1. Submarine volcanoes--Juvenile literature. 2. Volcanism--
Juvenile literature. 3. Islands--Juvenile literature. I. Title.
  QE521.3.T34 2008
  551.42--dc22
                    2008052652

Acknowledgments

The author and publishers are grateful to the following for
permission to reproduce copyright material: Alamy p. **16**
(Franco Salmoiraghi); Corbis pp. **23**, **26** and **27** (Ralph White);
Getty Images pp. **9** (Koichi Kamoshida), **13** (DEA/PUBBLI
AER FOTO), **15** (Art Wolfe); iStock pp. **19** (© 2007 Alberto
Pomares G.), **20** (© Dawn Nichols); istockphoto **background
image** (© Dean Turner); Photolibrary pp. **4** (Tammy Peluso),
7 (CARL ROESSLER), **11** (Gerald Nowak), **17** (Douglas
Peebles), **18** (Reinhard Dirscherl), **21** (Kevin Schafer), **22**
(Hjalmar Bardarson), **24** (Shaneff Carl), **29** (Chad Ehlers);
Science Photo Library p. **25** (ROYAL ASTRONOMICAL
SOCIETY).

Cover photograph of a volcanic eruption, Aetna, Italy (top)
reproduced with permission of Photoshot/©Westend61 and a
limestone island, Phang Nga National Park, Thailand (bottom)
reproduced with permission of Getty Images/National
Geographic/Jason Edwards.

Every effort has been made to contact copyright holders of
any material reproduced in this book. Any omissions will
be rectified in subsequent printings if notice is given to the
publisher.

Contents

Some words are shown in bold, **like this**. You can find out what they mean by looking in the glossary.

Underwater Mountains

Volcanoes are mountains, but they are very different from regular mountains. They may look like quiet mountains that never change. But hot **molten** (melted) rock called **magma** is lurking inside them.

Smoke rises from an erupting volcano in Papua New Guinea in Asia.

Suddenly, volcanoes can begin to rumble and **erupt**. Magma spurts out and becomes hot, molten rock called **lava**. Some volcanoes explode violently, with lava, gases, and clouds of ash shooting up into the sky. Other volcanoes quietly ooze out the molten rock, burning everything in the lava's path.

A volcanic island

This island formed from many volcanic eruptions under the ocean.

Volcanoes can be found all over Earth. Some rise high into the air. But there are many more volcanoes underwater. They sit on the ocean floor and may go unnoticed for a long time. But if an underwater volcano keeps erupting over and over for millions of years, its peak can eventually poke out of the water, forming an island.

An active island

The world's largest island that is almost entirely made up of **active** (still capable of erupting) volcanoes is Iceland, a country in the north Atlantic Ocean. Iceland formed millions of years ago from underwater eruptions.

What's Inside Earth?

The story of **volcanic islands** begins deep inside Earth, where layers of rock and metal are found at very high temperatures. At the center of it all is the **core**.

The core has two parts. The **inner core** is solid metal that sits at the center of Earth. Surrounding it is the **outer core**, which is made up of liquid iron.

Earth is made up of many layers.

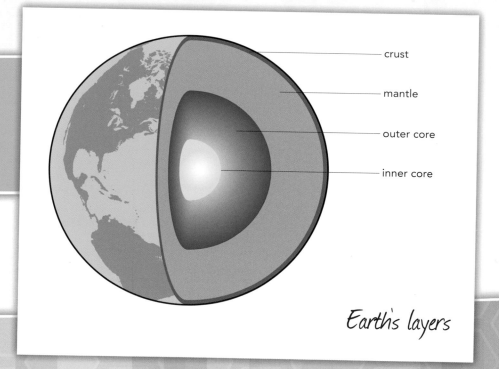

crust

mantle

outer core

inner core

Earth's layers

How big?

Earth's solid inner core is so large that it is almost the size of our moon! The fluid outer core is almost twice the size of the inner core.

The **mantle**, which sits on top of the core, is made of hot, semi-solid rock. We live on the **crust**, the outside layer of Earth. The crust is only a small part of Earth. Sometimes weak spots occur in the crust. Then the hot contents of lower layers can ooze out or force their way through to the top of the crust.

Lava and gases can ooze out of this weak spot in Earth's underwater crust.

7

Floating Land

The ground we stand on—Earth's **crust**—seems very solid and sturdy. But, in fact, the crust is divided into massive parts called **tectonic plates**. These huge plates of land float over Earth's **mantle**, moving a few inches each year. The plates go all around Earth. They fit together like a giant jigsaw puzzle.

Earth's tectonic plates

This map shows how Earth's tectonic plates fit together. The red triangles show where one plate is sliding under another.

Sometimes these huge plates can collide. As they continue pushing up against one another, the land has nowhere to go but up. When the plates are moving at different speeds, one plate may slide under the other.

In 2004 an earthquake caused dangerous cracks in this highway in Japan.

If two plates move in opposite directions, cracks in Earth's crust form. **Magma** can rise out of these cracks as the plates pull apart from one another.

Growing Mountains

When **tectonic plates** move, **magma** can rise, oozing out of Earth's **crust**. Two-thirds of Earth's crust is underwater. When magma spurts out into the ocean, the water cools it. As it cools, magma turns into hardened **lava**. Then more magma rises to the weak spot in Earth's crust. It flows on top of the hard lava from the last **eruption**.

More and more lava piles up underwater. Slowly, the mound of lava grows. After millions of years, the growing pile of hardened lava builds up into the shape of a mountain. As more eruptions occur, the underwater mountain grows taller and taller. Finally it reaches above the surface of the water. It becomes an island.

An underwater mountain grows with every volcanic eruption. After millions of years, it may become an island.

Underwater mountain

Many types of sea creature live on and around seamounts.

Under the sea

Underwater mountains are called seamounts. They are important because they provide a home for tiny ocean plants and animals called plankton, as well as many kinds of fish.

Kinds of Volcano

All **volcanoes** form from **eruptions** in Earth's **crust**. But they come in many different shapes and sizes. Sometimes **lava** flows very slowly out of an opening in Earth. Over thousands of years, many layers of lava build up. This forms a large, broad type of volcano called a **shield volcano**. Shield volcanoes have gently sloping sides.

Just resting?

When a volcano is not **actively erupting**, it is said to be **dormant**. But even if a volcano lies dormant for hundreds or even thousands of years, it could suddenly erupt.

Another type of volcano can form when **magma** shoots high into the air. Gas bubbles can get trapped inside the lava as it cools. These glassy pieces of lava are called cinders. When they pile up, they form a steep, small volcano called a **cinder cone**. Violent eruptions can create very large volcanoes called **composite cones**. These steep volcanoes are made from built-up layers of volcanic ash and lava.

Mount Vesuvius, Italy

Mount Vesuvius is a composite cone. It was created by violent eruptions.

Ring of Fire

A huge area, shaped like a giant horseshoe, surrounds the Pacific Ocean. It is called the **Ring of Fire** because there are hundreds of **volcanoes** all along this area. The Ring of Fire is also the source of many earthquakes. These earthquakes are caused by movements of Earth's **tectonic plates**. When these plates push together, pressure builds up. Earth's **crust** shakes when plates collide or separate with a violent movement. This leads to an earthquake.

The Ring of Fire spreads out around the Pacific Ocean.

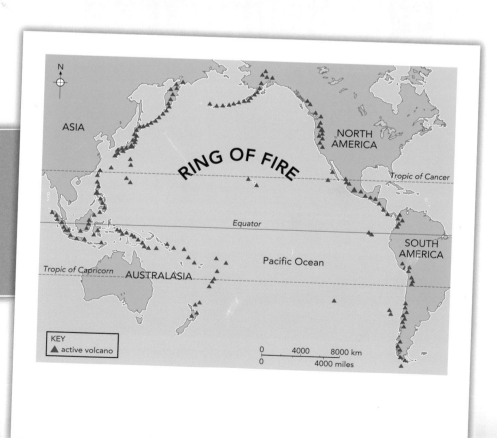

Indonesia, a country in Asia that is in the Ring of Fire, has 129 **active** volcanoes. The most active volcano in Indonesia is Mount Merapi, on the island of Java. Scientists watch this volcano very carefully because it could suddenly **erupt**. Tens of thousands of people live near the volcano. They could be killed if they are not warned in time.

Mount Etna, Sicily

Mount Etna shoots out fiery lava on the island of Sicily in Italy.

Fiery islands

Another area that is home to many volcanoes and **volcanic islands** is the Mediterranean Sea. Here, Mount Etna, on the Italian island of Sicily, is one of the most active volcanoes in the world. It is almost constantly erupting.

A Chain of Volcanoes

The Hawaiian Islands, in the Pacific Ocean, were formed when **magma** seeped out of Earth's **crust**. Hawaii sits above a **hot spot**—a part of Earth's **mantle** with a great deal of heat. When the portion of Earth's crust that covered the hot spot melted, **molten lava** shot up. An underwater **volcano** formed. When it reached the water's surface, it became the Hawaiian island of Kauai.

Mauna Kea

The top of Mauna Kea volcano in Hawaii is often covered in snow during winter.

Which mountain is taller?

Measured from sea level, Mount Everest, in Asia, is the tallest mountain in the world. But measured from its bottom in the ocean, Mauna Kea, a volcano in Hawaii, is taller than Everest.

Later, the **tectonic plate** over the hot spot moved. Kauai moved away from it. Another area of crust sat above the hot spot. This crust melted, and the lava broke through to form another island. Over millions of years, a chain of islands formed.

The largest island, called Hawaii, or the Big Island, is the youngest in the chain. It is still growing. Its currently **active** volcano, Kilauea, still spurts lava and adds more land to the island.

Kilauea volcano

Kilauea volcano shoots lava high into the air on Hawaii's Big Island.

An Island Home

When an underwater **volcano** first becomes an island, it is an empty, lonely place. But plants and animals eventually begin to live there.

New islands may be empty to begin with, but they do not stay that way forever.

Birds flying high in the sky may land on the new island. Birds' waste may contain seeds from the foods that they recently ate. These seeds may begin to grow in the island's soil.

Far away from the island, plants and animals might be swept into the ocean. They might swim or float to the island on a tree branch. They make a new home on the island. Soon plants and animals cover their new island home.

These palm trees might have grown out of coconuts from other islands.

Across the waves

Palm trees grow in tropical climates where it is hot and damp. Coconuts (the fruit of palm trees) can float many miles across bodies of water from one island to another. If the coconuts land in a good place with **fertile** soil (soil that helps them grow), they take root and grow in their new homes.

Strange Island Animals

The Galápagos Islands lie off the coast of South America in the Pacific Ocean. These islands were formed from undersea **volcanoes** created over a **hot spot**, much like the Hawaiian Islands were formed (see pages 16–17). Some of these plants and animals are found nowhere else in the world. Far away from other land, these creatures developed in strange ways.

The Galápagos Islands formed from volcanoes.

The Galápagos Islands

Marine iguanas can dive deep into the ocean looking for seaweed, their favorite food. Giant tortoises, up to 1.8 meters (6 feet) long, can live more than 100 years. A kind of Galápagos cactus grows as tall as a tree.

Rare Galápagos birds called **lava** gulls have dark bodies, but the insides of their mouths are bright red. Galápagos sea lions swim in the surrounding waters and also come up on shore.

When waved albatrosses are in love, they dance with each other.

Birds in love

Birds called waved albatrosses do not lay their eggs anywhere in the world outside the Galápagos Islands. They have a special mating dance. The birds bob their heads up and down. They make loud sounds like honking horns.

Fire in Iceland?

In 1963 a fisherman saw a strange sight. Smoke was rising from the water south of Iceland. The next day, a new **volcanic island** appeared in the water. The island was named Surtsey, after a giant from old Icelandic stories. The **volcano** kept **erupting** for a few more years. The small island has black volcanic sand.

The island of Surtsey formed from an underwater volcano.

Surtsey, Iceland

The end of an island?
Scientists say that the strong Atlantic Ocean waves, wind, and rain could slowly wear away the island of Surtsey. It could disappear in the next 100 years.

Large plant seeds that can survive in the Atlantic Ocean's salty water slowly floated onto Surtsey's shores. In the spring after Surtsey appeared, plants like sea grasses started to grow. Some plants floated on small clumps of grass from nearby islands. The wind brought dandelion seeds, which float on air. Years later, a group of seagulls settled on the island. They brought more seeds from plants like meadow buttercups.

Surtsey is now a home to plants and animals.

23

Danger!

Volcanoes can create **fertile** soil and become a good home for plants and animals like those on Surtsey. But volcanoes can also destroy lives. When an underwater volcano is building up, hot **lava** meets cold water. This can make the surface of the water explode. Boiling hot steam rises into the sky. Ocean water surrounding the volcano heats up. The water becomes dangerous, sending scalding hot waves to nearby shores.

Lava may appear harmless when it moves slowly. But lava is so hot that it can set fire to anything in its path. Lava flowing downhill can travel quickly, destroying whole valleys.

Hot lava flows and destroys a road on Hawaii's Big Island.

Volcanic lava on the move

Some volcanic gases are poisonous. Rocks and ash shooting out of volcanoes can travel far and destroy lives. When Mount St. Helens in Washington state **erupted** in 1980, it triggered the largest landslide in recorded history, destroying homes, bridges, and lives.

When Krakatoa volcano erupted in Indonesia, more than 36,000 people were killed.

A drawing of the eruption of Krakatoa

The sound of destruction

When Krakatoa, a **volcanic island** in Indonesia, violently erupted in 1883, thousands of people were killed. The sound of the explosion was so loud that people living thousands of miles away heard it!

Searching the Sea

The *Alvin* submersible goes exploring under the sea.

How do scientists study underwater **volcanoes**? They board underwater vessels called **submersibles** that can go deep into the ocean. They can get close-up views of volcanoes as they form on the ocean floor. In this way, scientists have explored an undersea volcano that is forming a new Hawaiian island in the Pacific Ocean. The future island is named Loihi. It is less than 1,000 meters (3,200 feet) below sea level. It could become an island about 250,000 years from now.

Smoking hot

In 1977 researchers entered a small submersible called *Alvin*. They went deep into the Pacific Ocean and discovered black smokers. These are a type of chimney-shaped vent, or crack in the ocean floor. Water from underneath Earth's **crust** shoots out of these vents. The water is very hot and rich in minerals, which plants and animals need to live and grow. Strange worms and giant clams live in these underwater black clouds.

A black smoker

If an area of the ocean is too deep or too dangerous for people to explore, scientists use Remotely Operated underwater Vehicles (ROVs). These are underwater robots that travel into deep ocean waters. An ROV has video cameras that send pictures to a ship waiting on the water's surface. Scientists in the ship operate an ROV by controlling its movements.

How Else Do Islands Form?

In addition to coming from **volcanoes**, islands can form in other ways. Some islands form when water rises, flooding low-lying land. Then only the highest mountain peaks stick out above the flood. These peaks become islands.

Rising water levels can turn high land and mountain tops into islands.

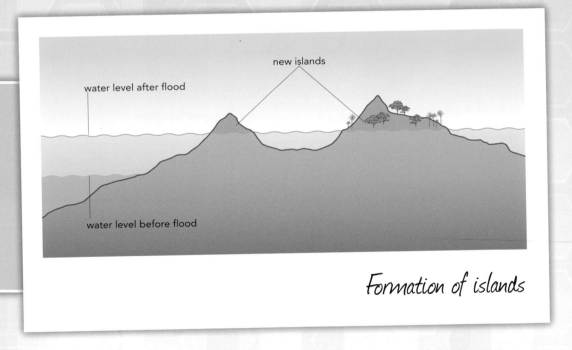

Formation of islands

Islands can also form when coral reefs grow around a **volcanic island**. A coral reef is made up of the skeletons of tiny animals called coral that live together. When some of the coral die, new ones live on top of the skeletons. Wind and waves gradually wear down the volcanic island. But if the coral keeps growing, an atoll forms.

An atoll is a coral island. An atoll is usually shaped like a circle. It surrounds a body of water called a lagoon.

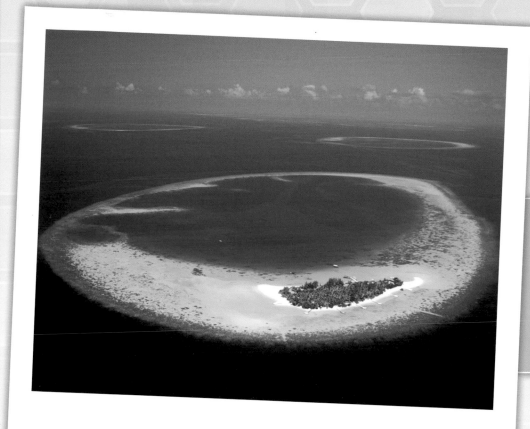

This atoll in the Indian Ocean was formed from coral.

A coral atoll

Islands of sand

Barrier islands are long, narrow strips of sand. They formed tens of thousands of years ago, during the Ice Age, when glaciers melted and carried sand and rocks to shallow areas.

Glossary

active currently erupting or showing signs that it will erupt

cinder cone small, steep volcano formed when magma shoots high into the air and falls back to Earth

composite cone large, steep volcano made from built-up layers of volcanic ash and lava, formed by violent volcanic eruptions

core center of Earth

crust outside layer of Earth

dormant not currently erupting but may erupt in the future

erupt when something that has been contained comes out forcefully. When a volcano erupts, it can shoot out lava, gas, and rocks.

eruption act of erupting, or coming out forcefully. The eruption of a volcano can involve explosions of lava, gas, and rocks.

fertile having what is needed for something to grow. Soil is fertile when it helps plants grow well.

hot spot super-hot part of Earth's mantle

inner core solid inside of the core (center) of Earth

lava hot, melted rocks that come out of a volcano

magma hot, melted rock that comes from inside Earth

mantle inside layer of Earth that sits on top of the core (the center)

molten melted

outer core outside of the core (center) of Earth. The outer core is made up of liquid iron.

Ring of Fire area surrounding the Pacific Ocean where hundreds of volcanoes are located. Many of the world's earthquakes occur there.

shield volcano large, broad volcano with gently sloping sides

submersible vessel that can go underwater

tectonic plate part of the crust, the top layer of Earth, that fits together with other plates like a big jigsaw puzzle. Tectonic plates are huge plates of land that float over a layer of Earth called the mantle.

volcanic island island that builds up when an underwater volcano keeps erupting and finally reaches above the water

volcano mountain with an opening where lava, gas, and rocks can shoot out

Find Out More

Books to read

Do you still have questions about volcanoes and islands? There is much more to learn about these fascinating topics. You can find out more by picking up some of these books from your local library:

Mason, Paul. *Into the Fire: Volcanologists (Scientists at Work)*. Chicago: Heinemann Library, 2008.

Townsend, John. *Earthquakes and Volcanoes: A Survival Guide (Earth Science)*. Chicago: Raintree, 2006.

Waldron, Melanie. *Volcanoes (Mapping Earthforms)*. Chicago: Heinemann Library, 2008.

Websites to explore

Find out whether what you've seen about volcanoes in the movies is true, learn about volcano scientists, and lots more on this government site:
http://volcanoes.usgs.gov/about

Take a virtual climb into a volcano's crater and play volcano games on this site:
http://volcano.oregonstate.edu/

Explore deep oceans and learn about creatures that live there:
www.extremescience.com/ocean-geography.htm

Index